Footprints in
the Sky

Footprints in the Sky

Shirley Smith

Library of Congress Control Number:		2019901163
ISBN:	Hardcover	978-1-7960-1330-6
	Softcover	978-1-7960-1329-0
	eBook	978-1-7960-1328-3

Print information available on the last page.

Rev. date: 02/21/2019

To order additional copies of this book, contact:
Xlibris
1-888-795-4274
www.Xlibris.com
Orders@Xlibris.com
791254

Lord put my footprints in the sky. Let me fly higher than any bird can fly. Lord let me soar like an eagle. Lord let me get to the mountain top with you. Lord let me tread upon your mighty waters. Let me drink from the fountain of truth and over flow with your goodness. Lord put my foot prints in the sky and take me higher than any bird can fly.

Is it the sun that makes the light or is it the moon that shines bright? It is god the light of the world. He is the light in all mankind. Is it the wind that blows or is it the breath of god that goes to and fro the earth. Is it thunder that you hear or is it the voice of god speaking loud and clear. Who is the one that spoke the world into existence? He is a mighty wonder.

A voice from Heaven, I hear a voice from heaven calling my name I hear a voice from heaven saying your prayers are not in vain. I hear a voice from heaven saying I am with thee

I hear a voice from Heaven saying you are set free because you believe in me. With GOD ALL THINGS ARE POSSIBLE.

A GLIMPSE OF HEAVEN, I know with one glimpse from heaven I will never be the same. One glimpse from heaven I will forever call your name. One glimpse from heaven I know your light will shine through me I know with one glimpse from heaven I know you will set me free from the stresses of the world. Lord you are amazing. One glimpse from heaven I will forever call out your name one glimpse from heaven I know you will poor out a blessing I can't contain. I know that your god and your mighty and true because you are the god that made the skies blue you are a mighty god and I love you.

Sleeping on a cloud lord let me sleep in peace lord let me awake with the fullness of your spirt lord let me start my day with praises and song and bring peace to my fellowman. Lord please let me be a help to someone today and bring the word of god in my heart to give to man and bring hope to the world lord let your holy spirit dwell with me forever.

Prayer, Lord I will seek your face daily lord clean me of all unrighteousness take me out of the valley of unforgiveness and bring me to an open door filled with your glory lord with you I know that you have all I need so lord make me over

make me new make me yours forever lord because I know your word is true.

Because I choose Jesus I AM FREE Because I choose Jesus I am redeemed, Because I choose Jesus I AM SAVED, Because I choose Jesus I AM FILLED WITH GODS holy spirit. Because I choose Jesus THE GREAT IAM KNOWS MY NAME!

Not an ordinary love. Lord your love is not ordinary. It's extraordinary! It's a love like I never known. Who can stand before you and not give you glory lord I glorify you. You are my life you are my love you are my god. Stay with me lord hold me in your arms. Open the door to eternity lord and send your light of love.

Create a protective barrier that no man can break. Read the word of god the word is everything that you need to keep you in perfect peace. Believe in the word of god and fight though life obstacles with his word. God will create a flame of fire between you and your enemies a supernatural barrier that no man can come through open your heart and let the Holy Spirit flow through your spirit and teach you god's way. The word of god says I am the way the truth and the life.

A Royal Priesthood. The Holy word says you are in Christ. A people for his own possession, that you may proclaim the excellences of him who called you out of darkness into his marvelous light.

Discovering the king in you. God always has a plan for your life. You are here for a purpose and you have a destination, a divine calling by God. In order to discover the king in you, you must put God first and he will show the divine order in which you shall go. Be not afraid of new ideas. A change of employment a move to a new location…it may be in God's divine will. Answer your calling and embrace what gifts God has given you. Walk in excellence before the almighty God, The King of the universe.

You are a queen. Hold your head up high. Look toward the sky and know that your help comes from the Lord. No matter where life takes you know that the Lord is on your side. Put God first and he will give you the strength to carry on and be the Queen he has made you and God will soon send your king. To give you the love that you need and always remember to look towards heaven for unanswered questions, things you may not understand because God knows all and

sees all. Know that God loves you most of all and he will fight your battles.

With the Lord I am an overcomer. I will stand up and do the will of him who is the great almighty. I will have a willing heart and accept what he has given me and glorify him always.

Lord you bring out the best in me lord I know you see more in me than myself when I am down you lift me up when I am afraid you sustain me when I am lonely you cover me with your love. When I am in trouble you take me to safety. Lord please lead me to an open path, full of your goodness, and give me your light of love.

Sound the trumpets! Blow the horns the almighty god will return believe in your heart that the lord walks with you trust that the lord walks with you know that god will take care of you all of your days honor him and bless him for he will return for his children.

Mind over matter when trouble arises bring the word of god to the battle field don't let your troubles get you down be lifted by god's word and carry the torch of a triumphant soldier.

When the storm clouds gather it looks like rain. Hold on god's children your prayers are not in vain. The lord will rain on you showers of goodness and mercy too and give you great joy in spite the flood that you may walk through. Be of good courage and diligence too. And walk in the ways of the lord you will make it through.

Walking in a field of happiness with you lord my days are brighter with you lord my nights are peaceful with you I am evolving through your wonder working power. Thank you lord for taking me to newer heights. Giving me guidance, and placing my feet at the door of great success.

Give me a light in a sea of darkness give me shelter from the rain give me hope lord for tomorrow and let the sun shine once again send an angel to give me a message of peace and let the flowers bloom in winter give me your hand lord to walk into a newness in you. Lord let your light shine until the end of time. Lord you are the beauty of love.

He's the god of restoration he's the god of new beginnings. We are the people of the most high god we must give gods light to the world show kindness and have adoration for the lord and show boldness in the lord demonstrate agape love have a giving heart and open your mind to receive what god

has put into our hearts Renew your mind today with the word of god and he will renew your strength in him.

Give me your hand lord to walk into a door of grace open my eyes to see the depth of your love grant me humility that I may have a humble sprit give me a light lord that shine so brightly in the earth so I may bring the gift of your holy word throughout the world.

Place your hand on my heart lord and fill it with your eternal love. Give me your warm embrace and cover me with your remarkable kindness.

With you Lord, I am an overcomer. I will stand uprightly and do the will of him who is the great almighty. I will have a willing heart and accept what he has given me. I will glorify you always. Heaven only knows how great and magnificent God is. Heaven awaits God's children entering. The time is near. Begin your journey. Walk to the path of all righteousness and do God's will!

Once God has spoken, it's done. Believe and trust in the almighty God. Know that he is God and God alone. There's no one greater or better to take care of your needs. Have faith that what you ask for he will give according to his will.

Imprint the word of God in your heart and always remember God has the world in his hand.

Can we hold fire in our hand without being burned? No. Can we count the stars and know the number of them? No Obey God. He is beyond great! He is beyond powerful! He is the God of supernatural EXCELLENCE!

Green Meadows. Walking in green pastures, take the time to smell the roses and marvel at God's beautiful world. Wait patiently for God's hand to move in your life. Believe in your heart that God walks with you through everything. Take the time to enjoy the blessings that God has given you and place your burdens at the master's feet. Give him glory each and every day. Psalms 23:2 "He makes me lie down in green pastures…"

Thank you Lord. You've been so good to me. When the sun is not shining, your love shines in my heart. When it's raining, you shower me with your love. When it's dreary, you bring sunshine to my spirit, and for that I say "Thank you" for a love that no man can give.

God's angels are among us. They camp all around us and protect us from harm. They are God's messengers. Delight yourself in God's word and let him manifest his love and his

awesome character in you and make you into the child of God he has called you to be. Believe that God's angels are with you and know that God will be our protector.

Walking in the ways of the lord. Keep straight don't turn back. Keep walking on god's road to victory. Keep praising him; keep praying you will get to paradise.

Sing praises to the lord for his love is every lasting. Give honor and glory to the most high god because he's worthy Look toward heaven and know that your heavenly father awaits your coming so believe in your heart that whatever stands in your pathway god can remove and you will be placed back to the road of glory.

Buried treasures there is buried treasures that the human eyes can't see there are things in life that can only be handled by god. Look no more for treasures on earth because your treasure will only be found in god. An eternal peace that can't be explained.

Crossing the river Jordon get ready children of god to cross over be strong and hold on be diligent and look up to the sky and know where your help comes from know that you will get to your destiny. Waters may be deep but gods hand can surely bring you to the surface.

Keep singing, Keep praying, keep praising keep loving, keep laughing and rejoicing for the king is coming soon. King Jesus.

We walk in divergent territories of the world seeking life's path to a greater being a greater conquest to live and to thrive in prosperity but we must know there's nothing done by our might or our strength but by the mighty hand of god. We as people are always looking everywhere but not putting our heads together brainstorming to bring equality and peace in the land. But instead always separating. Love has no color. So we as a people should look up to the most high god for

guidance and strength god rules the nations an all the world
and its splendor for it is gods glory not man.

The day time stood still God is a great wonder his love is
all real he put his hand in the sky and time stood still. His
hands are mighty and great his hands makes the earth quake
he is a mighty wonder to whom that is of god place your hand
in the master hand and let him show you things that are afar
far from the natural mind far from this world. But mysteries
of heaven mysteries of things that are not seen nor heard of
god's word is the key to our salvation renew your mind and
let god renew your heart and seek god's glory. The word says
Joshua 10:13 so the sun stood still and the moon stopped till
the nation avenged itself on its enemies.

We as a people should understand and know the problems
that we are facing at this time and hour is critical. Know that
god's mighty hand is on us great and small. HE SEES AND
KNOWS ALL AND HAVE A ULTIMATE PLAN FOR
US WE SIT AND PONDER on what shall come our way
in these last days but god only knows or future we must stay
prayerful and listen for gods holy spirit to speak and believe
that the lord will take care of his people but always remember
we must keep his statues and honor him at all times put him

first in our lives so that in this hour we will not be afraid of the terror or a thief in the night but know by gods might and strength we will be conquers and triumph over all our enemies but we must repent and be long suffering through any time of sorrow but we must hold on to gods holy word to be conquers, to be courageous to be fearless. Believe that god has the final say with all things. God is in control and there is no one that can take his place. Be of good courage.

Standing in a field of beautiful flowers the color of the flowers radiates god's beauty and glory. As the wind blows the flowers sway back and forth the beautiful aroma that release in the air is a fragrance of god's love to all mankind. Take the time to marvel at god's omnipotent glory and seek the beauty of the mind body soul and sprit. Through gods holy spirit.

A flower that never blooms. Don't let life pass you by step out on faith and do what god has called you to do. Live your dreams use the gifts god has given you for his glory and you will fly like an eagle through the clouds of glory. Press on; hold on to god's unchanging hand. And live out loud.

I look outside it looks like rain hold on god's children there's power in his name. Through god we can change things move mountains he will take us out of the mist of valleys and

sit us on a high mountain he will take us on a high mountain and around mighty seas and take our hurt and pain and put it under his feet. I looked outside I saw that the rain had ended because of his mighty mighty hand. Now there's a beautiful array of sunshine have faith and believe then he will hear you from heaven and you will receive his glory.

THE GREAT I AM SPEAKS; I AM GOD that opens the sea. I am the god who is mighty. I am the god that laid the foundations of the earth I am the god that put the moon up above I am the god that gives you love, I am the god that gives you snow and the rain. I am he that knows the stars by name. I am the god that makes the wind blows I am the god who knows all things great and small. I am the god that has it all in my mighty hand. Believe in the great and powerful I am.

When the wind blows your way it will bring blessings when the wind blows your way it will bring happiness when the wind blows your way it will bring grace when the blows your way know that it's the breath of the almighty god that made heaven and earth.

Never look back always go forward in life don't let your past be your present by holding on to things of the distance past. Behold and look up to know that God is a God of

restoration and admiration he will place the things that are holding you bound in outer darkness never to be looked upon again don't pick up yesterday's paper for today's news. You are a new creature in Christ Jesus and don't forget. The God that made heaven and earth is with you. Believe in the savior who have all our lives in his hand and preserves the hopes and dreams of all mankind.

Sitting in heavenly places, looking toward Gods heaven to proclaim liberty throughout the land walking carefully to the great door of great ambition to be a mighty warrior using Gods word as a sword to ward off all enemies. Placing ambiguous demeaning words of logic in its place and uncovering deceit and deception being a master mind of the good things that life has to offer. And bringing peace in the land placing all past hurts aside. And forgiving our enemies. Showing love by blessing those that are not kind. Putting God first in all that you do and opening a door of goodness so that there will be peace throughout the land.

We are the children of God that are on the battlefield raised up as Gods army of human soldiers with holy ghost power weathering the storms of life. Being transform into complete and perfected saints of the most high looking toward

heaven and receiving Gods instruction and walking with the sword of faith putting the puzzle of greatness in the earth by Gods hand defeating all enemies by Gods holy power. God is the hand of greatness whom the children of Gods calls father. He speaks to the hearts and spirit of his chosen people who will carry the torch of freedom. The circle of faith only comes by prayer supplication and reading Gods word. God is alive and has already won the war on the battlefield so we must continuously call on him and believe in our hearts he has made the stars and place them as lights in the sky and has called us to be triumphant. Glory to the God of heaven. He lives FOREVERMORE.

Be mindful what you say about others you may find yourself battling for the same ball look up and know god is still on the throne. Respect others privacy and tread lightly on the waters of accusations because the battle is not yours it's the lord. Don't be an accuser be a person that listens and chooses your battles wisely. Bless others and god will bless you.

Hiding in the secret places of god riding under the shadow of the almighty seeking god's omnipotent glory. Leaving a trail of success and uncovering all unforeseen attributes of the enemy. Looking toward heaven for answers and losing

all types of unforgiveness. The god of hope is all we need for success so put on the helmet of salvation and march toward the flag of freedom.

Walking in heavenly places seeking gods glory treading the water of his ever flowing love gazing into a sun that made by gods hand. Believing and knowing he's the god of hope and life the mysteries surrounds us of a god that's great in all his ways. God knows all mankind. His power is ever flowing forever evolving he has no end. The face of god is of the unknown but his love has no end pick up your bibles and encounter the god of greatness.

Lord keep me close to you and give me all of you. Lord please keep me in perfect peace let me climb the latter of great success and reach the highest star lord let me sail on the greatest seas and climb the highest mountain. Lord please take me on a journey filled with your glory so that I may have eternal life.

The perfect storm there will be trials that come. But when they come reach for the lords hands there will be stumbling blocks but reach for the lord's hand there will be mountains to climb but always reach for the lord's hand. He will pull you to safety.

I am in Christ Jesus and he is in me god will break the bondage off of your life and bring freedom in Christ Jesus liberty and love withholding all Power in his hand and unlocking the doors of freedom god is all we need for everlasting life so pick up a crown of gods undying love and place it upon your head and always remember gods in control of all things. Great and small.

Rivers and rivers of love. Meet me at the river of life lord give me a key to an abundant life so that I may spread abundance to others. Let me swim in your crystal rivers and come out clothed with diamonds to spread throughout the world. The diamonds are the words of god for your words are more than rubies and precious as any diamond ever known.

I have been in the wilderness but god touch my hand I didn't know how long I would be down but god helped me to stand I didn't know how far I had to travel but god took the wheel I even cried many tears but in my heart I heard peace be still So hold on when times are hard because. Gods still on the throne in the mist of your storm feel the rain drops let him wash your burdens away because gods hand is in the mist of it all. So when you are feeling blue know that god is

the one who will carry you through your storm and bring peace to you hold on gods beloved. Let him walk with you.

Because of his goodness we are free no longer bound to the things of this world but putting a foot forward in a march toward freedom life and liberty engaging in motivational teachings of gods holy word and being equipped to be human solders in a world of uncertainty but looking up to the most high for guidance and recognizing our faults and sin an repenting for all sins and knowing if we will repent god will make all things new and we will be forgiven. It is not a wonder of where. It's a privilege to be in god's holy presence and be in the mist of the things of god. The days of the coming of Christ is here. And nothing will stand in the way of god returning ever knee shall bow and every tongue will confess that Jesus is lord.

My past my present my future. Every day is a day of thanks giving when we open our eyes in the morning and we can see the sun it's a blessing. Don't lose sight on the important things. Serving god and doing his will live in the present not the past and look for a bright future in Jesus. Give god your hand and let him lead the way out of the past by his word.

Tick Toc on gods clock God ways are not our ways. God performs not on the worlds timing but in due time does he perform and always on time. The word says he never sleeps nor slumber. He has impeccable time. And great in all his ways. Tic Toc on god's clock For every season there's a reason to call on god and diligently wait on him.

PRAYERS

Please Lord bring your children to a sea of forgiveness. Let us see your glorious power, teach us to love one another and carry the badge of peace.

Place your hand on my heart, Lord and fill it with your eternal love. Give me your warm embrace and cover me with your remarkable kindness.

Love. Love is a powerful emotion that God has given us. We must know that God is love and he wants to enrich our thoughts with his holy word to receive him.

Lord you bring out the best in me. Lord I know you see more in me than myself. When I am down you lift me up. When I am afraid you sustain me. When I am lonely you cover me with your love. When I am in trouble you take me to safety. Lord, please lead me to an open path full of your goodness and give me your light of love.

Hold me in your arms Lord, and please don't let me go. Take me to your living waters and let me drink from the fountain of peace. Open the door to your everlasting glory and give me your grace.

When there's a storm, God will be there to shelter you. God will place his hand upon you and give you all the love you want and need. The Lord will teach you how to Love your enemies and bless those that curse you. Put God first in your heart and he will grant you the power to overcome. Believe in the God of hope.

Standing by an open stream. Lord please take me to a fountain overflowing with success. Grant me your love and kindness to place in my heart. Lord please give me the wisdom that I need for life's journey.

Lord open the door and let grace and mercy step in lord give me the grace to walk in your ways and give me mercy lord when I call on you and put me in a secret place in your arms Lord please forgive me for my sin lord take me to a place filled with your love open the doors of heaven and pour out a blessing on your children and please lord guide me through the path of all righteousness.

Lord help your children. Forgive us father, for we have all sinned and fallen short of your glory. Make us new. Bring us to the valley of forgiveness so that we can enter into your kingdom. Give us a light that shines so brightly it takes us to your everlasting glory. Lord, help your children receive freedom in you.

Lord, bring your children to a sea of forgiveness. Let us see your glorious power. Teach us to love one another and carry the badge of peace.

THE GREATEST GIFT. The greatest gift I have ever received was you Lord. Your love stands the test of time. Your beauty is timeless and divine. Your love is like a love I never known. Place me by your doorstep Lord and let me enter into the greatest love ever known to mankind.

Lord, please forgive me. I have fallen short of the glory cleanse me purify my soul and spirit. Unlock the chains that keep me bound and fill it with you glory and divine nature. Cleanse me of all unrighteousness and set me free!

When man says no God says yes no matter what door have closed know that God has a better plan don't be discouraged

or dismayed. The king of glory will comfort you through the mist of your troubles God will open a window of peace and let you drink from the fountain of living waters he will pour goodness and mercy in your spirit and shower you with his love. He is the great I am.

When things you don't understand, reach for Lords hand when you are in sinking sand reach for the Lord's hand. When your troubles are over flowing, reach for the Lord's hand. When there's no open door. Reach for the Lord's hand you will be lifted to a place of safety.

Lord, don't let me walk in muddy waters let me walk upon the earth with your strength and immaculate grace upon my life. Let your wonder working power overtake me to walk in yours ways and walk in your divine will.

When I close my eyes at night lord please hold me tight in your arms. Take me to a place of good sleep and peace open up the gates of heaven and pour out your love that never ends let me awake with the song of your wonder working power and give me a touch of your divine grace.

Take a leap of faith and venture out into a new discovery of life, love and happiness. Take a peek into the unknown

windows of God believing and putting all your trust in him. Open up his everlasting doors and walk into total greatness.

Lord give me springtime in winter lord surround me with your love give me hope for tomorrow and send a dove to fly Over your skies so that I will remember your everlasting love.

Morning glory wake up in the morning with song in your heart thanking the most high for a another day knowing that he will pave the way to a greater outlook on life you have never heard of be thrilled to know that god will guide you in the direction of happiness and his knowledge open doors man can't shut and bring you to a place of great success. Believe in him and receive his glory.

Lord you are the air that I breathe you are every holy dance that I dance you are divine. You are my king you are my god.

Tender mercies Please give me your tender mercies lord and sit me upon your highest mountain open the door to freedom and take me to the mercy seat of god let me take a look into the heavens and always remember your beautiful kingdom so that I will have a peace of heaven in my heart.

Lord your light keeps me going even when I want to give up your love keeps me flowing even when I can't see my way

out lord your word is an ever flowing stream that gives me strength lord I know I don't have to fight the battle because the battle is already won.

Catch my tears lord hold them in your mighty hand and remember me take me to a place with over flowing success and bring me to your mighty waters give me a key to abundant life so I may impart abundance of blessing to others.

Lord will you touch my hand lord take me to your promised land lord I know I can trust you I know that you will walk me through my cloudy days I know that you have the key to a prosperous life so lord please touch my hand and bring me to your promised land.

Lord your peace has bestowed on my heart your love has incrusted in my every being your grace has planted in my life my tears have come up to you as a stream that runs overflowing to your throne of living waters. You have given me the strength to conquer the tests of life. I am yours lord for eternity.

Meet me at heaven's gate lord and unlock your divine wisdom. Meet me at heaven's gate lord and bring knowledge and understanding meet me at heaven's gate lord and bring

me obedience to your will that will carry me through life incredible journeys.

Love Letter to Jesus. My love. My life my hands are ready for the giving of the greatest love that ever lived my heart is overwhelmed with your love and your grace has been poured on me like an ever flowing stream. Your word is like fresh manna from heaven. Lord please give me the sweetest flower in the field with the sweetest fragrance and let me sing of your glory all of the day may the love of God be my portion and the love of God be my peace, glory to the God of Zion, glory to the God of heaven and earth. Make this earth proclaim your glory throughout the land.

As the eagle fly to the sunset yet will I fly to you lord give me your hand and lead the way to a beautiful life in Jesus Christ unlock the sacred doors to an everlasting love and impart your wisdom in me. Please lord, hold my hand but yet set me free from sin.

Lord place your hand in mine give me your light and live in me take me to a sacred place in you full of your majesty. Create in me a clean heart and a right sprit. Make me yours forever and place me at the doorway of happiness. Let me stand on the steps of heaven and walk to you.

When storms arise read the word of god it will put you at ease and bring you to a plateau of great peace. Heaven is at hand, reach up to the sky and call on Jesus and remember he hears us when we call out to him. Believe in your heart that he will return for his beloved children.

Lord place me at the throne of god give me the wisdom to know your ways guide my footsteps to an open door of success and place me on solid ground give me a link to follow so that I will walk towards the mark of greatness and put a crown of pure old on my head. Give me your hand precious lord and make me yours forever. Forever in glory. The devil is already defeated gods hand is the one and only one that can save us that can bring us to a place of promise a place of hope. A place of change. If there was an open door full of gods promises would you walk through? Or would you wait for man to give you permission? Obey god and look toward heaven for answers to things that are not under stood. Jesus is the answer. Believe in god and establish new mindsets of living. Loving and bring good tidying to all mankind.

Welcome, welcome holy spirit. You are welcome in this place welcome, welcome Holy Spirit. I feel your warm embrace. Walk with me lord as I walk in life talk for me

lord as I bring good tidings to my fellow man give me your hand and lead me to freedom. Place me at the fountain of youth and give me strength to carry the torch of greatness. Welcome, welcome holy spirit in this earthen vessel.

Planting a seed of righteousness and unlocking sacred doors of success establishing good friendships and exalting the almighty god is a key ingredient in today's life lessons. Believing that and knowing that all of gods ways are perfect and without blemish the word say his ways are not our ways his thoughts not our thoughts. We must come to common ground in the spectrum of his word and listen to reason and believe in our heart his word is true and complete and will stand the test of time and know that he's almighty

There is a place where flowers are forever blooming and there's always light and never darkness. The seas are crystal clear. And the streets are paved in gold. Where there's no sickness or disease a place dreams are reality. And the love of god never ends. A place where there is no time but gods forever flowing stream of love let god embrace you and take you to a higher place in him so that one glorious day we will be caught up in glory never to bewildered again. God never

changes speak life and live more abundantly in Jesus Christ the word says above all things acknowledge him.

When the wind blows who knows what will come your way. Life is full of challenges we must keep prayer in our lives put god first and walk towards forgiveness an believe that god will restore the things that we've lost look up to the sky and know that Jesus will always be there to guide us.

A brazing alter come to the alter with your hands held high tell the lord your problems and reach for the sky. Look up to heaven and call his name he is the god that will put the devil to shame. He is god yes it is so he is the one who make the winds blow through the earth give god all the praise for he is the one to turn your midnight into days. Reach up and call god's name and know that the blessings of god is only a prayer away. The word of god says he's great in all his ways. The word is true and won't return unto him void.

A checkered past don't let your past be your present take control of your thought life with the word of god. God can and will restore you of past mistakes. Believe in god magnificent power and trust him with all that you have place your problems at his feet and he will rain his glory over you

and heal your body soul and mind. Be encouraged be blessed and be a triumph solider in Christ Jesus.

Help me lord the wind is raging but god is in control. The lightning is flashing but gods hand made it all the sand is knee deep but the lord will sustains me. Help me lord through these trying times and lift me out of my shame. Glory to your name lord. Glory to your name.

River of tears lord I cry a river of tears before you. Lord keep me close to your heart never let me go guide my steps into your marvelous light. Lord wipe my tears with your mighty hands and bring the love of god in my heart. Take me to that sacred place in god that's never been known and give me the keys to a righteous life.

Lord I am sorry I repent of my sin. Lord you know my innermost thoughts you fashioned me in my mother's womb. Lord place me at the doorstep of repentance and bring me a staff of integrity and strength to fight against all enemies. There's a battle of mind that most men may not understand but with all things must be brought to god in prayer. I believe your divine nature dwells within my spirit and you have the key. I am overwhelmed with sadness for my sin but I know you will lift me higher than I ever been lifted now that I have

been through the fire and the rain I am stronger and wiser thankyou father for your mercy and kindness and most of all thank you for your son.

Be a believer you are more than a conquer through Jesus our savior. Pull back the curtains of unbelief and open the door to faith. In Christ Jesus look up and count the stars AND REMEMBER GOD MADE THEM ALL. Take gods hand and let him lead the way to freedom in Christ. Walk into a valley of love and happiness and uplift the master on high he will bring you out of the valley of sin into his marvelous light. Take the time to study his word and walk toward the mark of his everlasting glory. He will pick up the pieces that have been broken in your heart and place them back together. You will be healed delivered and set free. And remember his name in the midnight hour and exalt the word of the almighty god. Have hope and believe.

When the wind blow who knows what it will bring is there a storm brewing or will the east winds bring hope in the world of uncertainty. Surely god knows what will come our way EVEN WHEN THINGS SEEM NOT TO BE GOING The way we planned look up and know that god is great in all his ways. Remember his name on high and know

that he will protect and perfect which is his. Our god is the omnipotent one. The god of all heaven and earth.

Lord let me tread on a sea of diamonds. Let me climb the highest mountain let me walk the walk of a triumphant solider and bring a light that shines all through your world for your glory. Glory to the one and only god.

Will you be ready? Have you done what's required have you been chosen for the task of preaching the gospel of Jesus Christ? Will candles be burned at both ends or will the fire be lit with the flame of the almighty. Will you walk in integrity or will you walk in dismay. Let god be the lifter of your head and bring you to his brazing alter.

Take me across the dessert and many seas let me smell the roses of success and be yours in grace unlock the secret treasure and pen me with honor give me a scepter of a queen and wisdom to always have your word in my mouth. Unlock the sacred door to the mind and impart your wisdom in my heart. Lord you are my life. You are my god for eternity. The love I have for you is unspeakable for the love I have for you is like no other love I have ever known.

We walk by faith and not by sight we must stand firm on his word and look toward the heavens for answers paving

the way for others who believe in Christ Jesus and breaking the chains of unbelief walking toward the mark of great accomplishments. And lending a helping hand, to your fellow man that is in need. The word of god in its entirety is the key to problem solving Jesus has the answer to all problems. God has great THINGS ahead gods promises are true and will stand forevermore for he is great IN ALL HIS Ways. When god is with you. You will walk in your destiny.

He holds the sun in one hand the moon in another he is all powerful almighty he is the one and true god of the universe. One touch from him who sits on high will change your life and will bring you to a Plateau of greatness with reward. open up your bibles and get to know. The greatest love of all.

THERES A SHIFT IN the atmosphere ever time lord you are near. The Earth quakes the mountains shake. THE sea rumbles there's a shift in the atmosphere every time you near. THE EARTH AND ALL its spender belongs to you lord. Your hand is great upon the earth. YOU'RE MAJESTY UNKNOWN. The power that you obtain is divine and eternal. Your mercy is man saving grace. Lord you are magnificent and plenteous extraordinary power.

Riding on the wings of god. Have you ever been in a place where there was no way to turn look up problems solved there's a god that can solve any problem is there anything to hard for god? Remember who made heaven and earth. The one who made the ultimate sacrifice Jesus is lord he is the savior there's nothing or no one as powerful as he. Sing in your heart a new song of god's glory and he will direct your path.

Embrace the light of god in your life his holy spirit will create a new you in Christ Jesus. Read god's word and magnify his name. The light of god dwells within us and sets us free. Give god your all today tomorrow may be too late.

Let the tear drops fall where they may. Lord let the tear drops fall onto your throne so you may see my pain and sorrow please sweep my house clean and uncover my sins before you and wash them away. Take my hand precious lord and lead me to crystal clear waters so that I may see my reflections so that I may correct all imperfections' of the heart lead me to a pathway of righteousness' for your name sake and infuse love hope happiness and forgiveness in my heart give me a love for others and crown me with your honor and grace from above. Lord take me to a stream of happiness and

unlock the chains that are keeping me bound your love lord is all I need for the future.

Lord please forgive me for my sin take the stumbling blocks that are before me out of the way loose these chains. Create a right heart and mind in me. Give me the breast plate of righteousness. And take me to your forever flowing waters.

Lord help me through the desert spring forth water from the springs of heavens pour it into my life, Give me a torch for the knight light and give me your hand to place in mine. Walk with me lord until the sun shine again. Give me fresh cut flowers from a vine of roses.

Reach for a shooting star no matter how far glaze into a periscope with spiritual eyesight believe in your heart that a new day is dawning. And that gods light is all we needing. Put on the whole armor of god and walk toward the mark of greatness. Let gods light lead you to a room of excellence. Cast all your cares on him and always speak the word of god over any given situation. The word of god says they shall walk and not faint.

Lord my life is in your hands my heart is overflowing with uncertainty. I am weary in my thinking because of the issues that has been brought fourth. But I know your hand

will lift me up and your grace will carry me through you are my strength lord give me a light lord that shines through my heartache give me hope for tomorrow. I know that your love conquers all Lord you are my life.

A point of treasure seeks no more for treasure is in you. Give god your all place your troubles at his feet. Read god's word. And believe what he says is true. Walk up a stairway of peace and joy and exalt the word of god.

Greater is he that walks with mankind. Greater is he who is divine greater is he who makes the wind blows greater is he who knows your name. Can light a flame in the sky. A sun that never dims that will rise every morning and sets every evening who is the great I am. The brightest star of all gleaming from a piercing sun. The glory of him that sits on high is the ultimate author and finisher. Greater is he who makes the birds fly. Greater is he that made the sky and walks on a cloud, saying out loud, "arise all who is of God, I have it all in my mighty hands." He will never leave you or forsake you.

GO CHILDREN OF GOD AND PROCLAIM LIBERTY THROUGHOUT THE WORLD!